MICHELE ALTOBELLO

Easy Team Building

Activities to Inspire Creativity, Cooperation and Communication

Copyright © 2024 by Michele Altobello

All rights reserved. No part of this publication may be reproduced, stored or transmitted in any form or by any means, electronic, mechanical, photocopying, recording, scanning, or otherwise without written permission from the publisher. It is illegal to copy this book, post it to a website, or distribute it by any other means without permission.

Michele Altobello asserts the moral right to be identified as the author of this work.

Michele Altobello has no responsibility for the persistence or accuracy of URLs for external or third-party Internet Websites referred to in this publication and does not guarantee that any content on such Websites is, or will remain, accurate or appropriate.

Designations used by companies to distinguish their products are often claimed as trademarks. All brand names and product names used in this book and on its cover are trade names, service marks, trademarks and registered trademarks of their respective owners. The publishers and the book are not associated with any product or vendor mentioned in this book. None of the companies referenced within the book have endorsed the book.

First edition

This book was professionally typeset on Reedsy.
Find out more at reedsy.com

Contents

1	Introduction	1
2	The First Steps to Team Building	4
	Analyze Your Team: Are They in Person or Virtual?	5
	Select The Best Activity for Your Team	8
	Review The Instruction with Your Team	10
	Perform The Activity	13
3	Icebreakers	18
	Adjective + Name	19
	Two Truths & One Lie	19
	Introduction Bingo	20
	The Memory Test	21
	Minefield	22
4	Team Building Activities to Promote Communication	24
	Can You Hear Me Now?	25
	Blind Drawing	26
	Active Listening	27
	Spread The Word	27
	Role Play	28
5	Team Building Activities to Promote Cooperation	30
	Visit An Escape Room or Create a Virtual Escape Room	31
	Deserted Island	32
	Question and Answer Board	33
	Scavenger Hunt	34
	Movie Quote Trivia	34
6	Team Building Activities to Inspire Creativity	36

	Building Block Challenge	37
	Paper Plane Contest	38
	Team Goals Collage Board	39
	What's in the Box	39
	Back to the Old Drawing Board	40
7	Conclusion	42
8	References	44

1

Introduction

In today's fast-paced work environment, the success of an organization relies heavily on the strength and cohesion of its teams. A team that communicates effectively, collaborates well, and sparks creativity can achieve remarkable results. If you're looking to transform a group of individuals into a high-performing, united team, you're in the right place.

Welcome to *Easy Team Building: Activities to Inspire Creativity, Cooperation and Communication*. My name is Michele Altobello, and with over 20 years of experience as a nurse leader, I've seen firsthand how crucial effective team dynamics are for achieving success. My goal with this book is to offer you practical, easy-to-follow strategies for building stronger, more engaged teams. I believe that team building isn't just about organizing fun activities; it's about creating an environment where everyone can thrive, innovate, and work together seamlessly.

This book is designed to be your go-to resource for team building. Traditional team-building methods often involve generic activities that might not meet the specific needs of your team. This guide is different. It offers a variety of activities tailored to help you enhance communication, foster cooperation, and spark creativity within your team. Whether you're leading a new team or looking to reinvigorate an existing one, you'll find valuable insights and actionable steps here.

Here's a quick overview of what you'll find in the chapters ahead:

- **The First Steps to Team Building** – Before you dive into activities, it's important to lay a solid foundation. This chapter will walk you through analyzing your team's needs, selecting the right activities, reviewing instructions clearly, and carrying out the activities smoothly. These steps are crucial for making sure your team-building efforts are effective and engaging.
- **Icebreakers** – Icebreakers are a great way to start off on the right foot. They help team members get to know each other, set a relaxed tone, and break down initial barriers. You'll find five engaging icebreaker activities in this chapter that are perfect for kicking off your team-building sessions.
- **Team Building Activities to Promote Communication** – Good communication is the backbone of a successful team. This chapter presents five activities designed to improve how your team conveys ideas, listens to one another, and collaborates. Strengthening communication will build a strong foundation of trust and understanding.
- **Team Building Activities to Promote Cooperation** – Cooperation is essential for achieving shared goals and creating a supportive work environment. Here, you'll discover five activities that encourage teamwork, mutual support, and collaborative problem-solving, helping your team work together more effectively.
- **Team Building Activities to Inspire Creativity** – Creativity drives innovation and keeps your team adaptable and forward-thinking. This chapter introduces five activities that will help your team unleash their creative potential and approach problems from new

INTRODUCTION

angles.

Each chapter is designed to be straightforward and easy to implement, so you can quickly integrate these activities into your team's routine. The goal is to provide you with practical tools that make a real difference in how your team performs and interacts.

As you go through this book, I encourage you to embrace the activities with an open mind and a willingness to explore new approaches. The strategies and exercises included here are meant to be flexible and adaptable to your team's unique needs. Effective team building is about more than just completing a single activity; it's about creating an environment where communication, cooperation, and creativity can thrive.

Let's start by setting the stage for successful team building. In the next chapter, we'll cover the essential first steps you need to take before launching into team-building activities. You'll learn how to analyze your team's needs, choose the best activities, review instructions clearly, and execute the activities effectively.

Thank you for picking up this guide. I'm excited to help you build a more connected, creative, and cooperative team. Let's dive in and get started!

2

The First Steps to Team Building

Before diving into the various team building activities, it's essential to lay a solid foundation. The success of any team building exercise hinges on the preparation and initial steps taken before the activity even begins. This chapter will guide you through the crucial first steps to ensure a smooth and effective team building experience.

Analyze Your Team: Are They in Person or Virtual?

Before embarking on any team building activity, it's crucial to understand the nature of your team. Are they working together in person, or are they spread across various locations and connecting virtually? Each setup presents unique challenges and opportunities, and recognizing these differences will help you tailor your approach for maximum effectiveness.

In-Person Teams

Benefits:

- **Direct Interaction:** In-person teams benefit from direct, face-to-face interaction. Non-verbal cues, such as body language and facial expressions, enhance communication and foster a deeper sense of connection.
- **Immediate Feedback:** Responses and feedback are immediate, allowing for real-time adjustments and a more dynamic exchange of ideas.
- **Hands-On Activities:** Physical presence allows for a wider range of team building activities, including those that involve movement, physical objects, and direct collaboration.

Challenges:

- **Scheduling:** Coordinating a time that works for everyone can be difficult, especially in larger teams or those with varying schedules.
- **Physical Space:** Finding a suitable location that can comfortably accommodate the entire team and the planned activities might be a logistical challenge.

Virtual Teams

Benefits:

- **Flexibility:** Virtual team building activities can be more flexible in terms of scheduling. Team members can participate from any

location, reducing the need for travel and physical presence.
- **Diverse Tools:** A variety of digital tools and platforms are available to facilitate virtual team building, offering creative ways to engage team members through video calls, chat, and interactive software.
- **Inclusivity:** Virtual activities can often be more inclusive, accommodating team members who might have physical limitations or other constraints that make in-person participation challenging.

Challenges:

- **Technical Issues:** Connectivity problems, software glitches, and varying levels of tech-savviness can hinder the smooth execution of virtual activities.
- **Limited Non-Verbal Communication:** Virtual interactions lack the richness of in-person communication. Non-verbal cues are harder to read, and the potential for misunderstandings can increase.
- **Engagement:** Keeping team members engaged and focused can be more challenging in a virtual environment, where distractions are just a click away.

By thoroughly analyzing your team, you can better anticipate these challenges and leverage the benefits. This understanding allows you to select activities that are most likely to succeed given your team's unique dynamics, setting the stage for effective and enjoyable team building experiences.

Select The Best Activity for Your Team

Selecting the right activity for your team is a pivotal step in ensuring the success of your team building efforts. The key is to match the activity to the specific needs and dynamics of your team, whether they are in person or virtual. Here, we will explore which types of activities work best in each context and how to make the most of them.

In-Person Activities

In-person teams have the advantage of physical presence, which opens a wide range of engaging and interactive activities.

Types of Activities:

- **Physical Challenges:** Activities like obstacle courses, scavenger hunts, or sports can be highly effective. These activities not only promote teamwork and cooperation but also provide a fun and energetic break from the usual work routine.
- **Workshops:** Hands-on workshops, such as art projects or problem-solving exercises, allow team members to collaborate closely and build stronger relationships.
- **Trust Exercises:** Activities designed to build trust, such as blindfolded navigation tasks, can be very impactful in person, where physical presence enhances the sense of vulnerability and reliance on teammates.

Benefits:

- **Enhanced Communication:** Face-to-face interaction allows for clearer communication, with the added context of body language and facial expressions.
- **Immediate Feedback:** Team members can give and receive immediate feedback, which helps in quickly addressing any issues or misunderstandings.
- **Stronger Bonds:** Shared physical experiences often lead to stronger interpersonal connections and a deeper sense of camaraderie.

Virtual Activities

Virtual teams can leverage digital tools to create engaging and interactive experiences that bridge physical distance.

Types of Activities:

- **Online Games and Challenges:** Virtual escape rooms, trivia contests, and online team challenges can be very engaging. These activities encourage problem-solving and teamwork in a fun, competitive environment.
- **Virtual Workshops:** Digital platforms can host various interactive workshops, such as virtual art tutorials or professional development sessions, allowing team members to collaborate and learn new skills together.
- **Icebreakers and Social Hours:** Virtual coffee breaks, happy hours, or icebreaker sessions help team members connect on a personal level, fostering a sense of community and belonging.

Benefits:

- **Flexibility:** Virtual activities offer greater flexibility in terms of scheduling and participation. Team members can join from anywhere, making it easier to accommodate different time zones and locations.
- **Cost-Effective:** Many virtual activities are less expensive than their in-person counterparts, eliminating the need for travel and venue costs.
- **Inclusivity:** Virtual settings can be more inclusive for team members with physical limitations or other constraints that might make in-person activities challenging.

When selecting the best activity for your team, consider the specific goals you want to achieve. Are you aiming to improve communication, foster cooperation, or inspire creativity? Also, consider the preferences and personalities of your team members. Activities should be inclusive and engaging for everyone, ensuring that all team members feel comfortable and motivated to participate.

By carefully choosing activities that align with your team's structure and objectives, you can create meaningful and enjoyable team building experiences that promote stronger bonds, better communication, and enhanced cooperation, regardless of whether your team is in person or virtual.

Review The Instruction with Your Team

Before diving into any team building activity, it's essential to ensure that every team member fully understands the instructions. Clear and thorough instruction sets the stage for a successful activity by minimizing confusion, aligning everyone with the activity's goals, and fostering a sense of readiness and confidence among participants.

Importance of Clear Instructions

- **Minimize Confusion:** Clear instructions help eliminate misunderstandings and ambiguities. When everyone knows what is expected, the activity can proceed smoothly without unnecessary interruptions or the need for constant clarifications. This is particularly important for activities with complex rules or multiple steps, where even a small misunderstanding can disrupt the flow and effectiveness of the exercise.
- **Align with Goals:** Team building activities are designed with specific objectives in mind, such as enhancing communication, fostering cooperation, or sparking creativity. Thoroughly reviewing the instructions helps ensure that all participants understand these goals and how the activity will help achieve them. This alignment keeps everyone focused and motivated, enhancing the overall impact of the exercise.
- **Foster Readiness and Confidence:** When team members clearly understand what they are supposed to do, they are more likely to engage fully and participate actively. Confidence in knowing the rules and objectives reduces anxiety and hesitation, allowing participants to immerse themselves in the activity and contribute their best efforts.

Steps to Review Instructions

1. **Explain the Purpose:** Begin by explaining the purpose of the activity. Discuss the goals and expected outcomes, and how the activity fits into the broader context of team building. This helps team members see the value and relevance of the exercise, increasing their engagement and commitment.
2. **Break Down the Steps:** Break down the instructions into clear, manageable steps. Use simple language and avoid jargon or overly complex terms. If the activity involves multiple stages or roles, explain each part in detail and ensure everyone knows their specific responsibilities.
3. **Use Visual Aids:** Visual aids, such as slides, diagrams, or videos, can enhance understanding. Visuals help clarify complex instructions and provide a reference that team members can revisit if they have questions during the activity.
4. **Encourage Questions:** Create an open environment where team members feel comfortable asking questions. Encourage them to seek clarification on any points they do not fully understand. Addressing questions upfront prevents confusion and ensures everyone is on the same page.
5. **Conduct a Dry Run:** For particularly complex activities, consider conducting a dry run or walkthrough. This practice session allows team members to familiarize themselves with the process and ask questions in a low-pressure setting. It also helps identify any potential issues or misunderstandings that can be addressed before the actual activity begins.

Benefits of Thorough Instruction Review

- **Smooth Execution:** Clear instructions lead to smooth execution. When team members understand the activity thoroughly, they can focus on participating and collaborating rather than trying to figure out what to do next. This maximizes the activity's effectiveness and allows everyone to derive the most benefit from it.
- **Increased Engagement:** Team members who understand the instructions are more likely to engage fully and enthusiastically. They feel confident in their roles and responsibilities, which encourages active participation and a positive attitude towards the activity.
- **Enhanced Learning:** When participants understand the activity and its objectives, they are more likely to absorb the lessons and insights it offers. Clear instructions help team members connect the activity to real-world applications, reinforcing the skills and concepts being practiced.

By taking the time to thoroughly review the instructions with your team, you set the stage for a successful and impactful team building activity. Clear, comprehensive guidance ensures that everyone is aligned, confident, and ready to engage, paving the way for meaningful interactions and valuable outcomes.

Perform The Activity

With your team well-prepared and informed, it's time to perform the activity. The execution phase is where the planning and preparation come to life. Conducting the activity in a structured and organized manner ensures that everyone remains engaged and that the objectives are met. Here's how to effectively carry out the team building exercise, along with tips for maintaining engagement and recognizing signs of disengagement.

- **Structure and Organization:** Start by clearly outlining the activity's structure. Remind team members of their roles and the steps involved. Maintain a timeline to ensure the activity progresses smoothly and stays within the allotted time. This structure helps keep everyone focused and on track.
- **Facilitation:** As the facilitator, your role is to guide the activity, monitor participation, and intervene when necessary. Be observant and ready to provide support, answer questions, and address any issues that arise. Facilitation is about balancing guidance with allowing the team to work through the activity organically.
- **Observation:** Keep a close eye on the dynamics of the group. Watch for signs of engagement and disengagement and be prepared to adjust your approach as needed. Active observation helps you identify when the activity is flowing well and when intervention is needed to keep everyone on track.

Signs of Disengagement

- **Lack of Participation:** One of the most apparent signs of disengagement is a lack of participation. Team members might be quiet, hesitant to contribute, or appear uninterested. In virtual settings, this might manifest as team members turning off their cameras or not participating in chats.
- **Body Language:** In in-person settings, body language can be a clear indicator of disengagement. Signs include crossed arms, lack of eye contact, slouching, or looking at phones or other distractions. In virtual settings, team members might appear distracted or not

attentive to the screen.
- **Negative Attitude:** A negative attitude can also signal disengagement. This might include reluctance to participate, negative comments, or a general lack of enthusiasm. Such attitudes can spread and affect the overall morale of the group.
- **Side Conversations:** Side conversations, whether in person or via private messages in a virtual setting, can indicate disengagement. These distractions pull focus away from the main activity and can disrupt the flow and cohesion of the group.

Tips to Keep Everyone Engaged

1. **Set Clear Expectations:** At the outset, set clear expectations for participation. Encourage everyone to contribute and explain the value of their engagement. Clear expectations help create a sense of responsibility and involvement.
2. **Mix Up Activities:** Use a variety of activities to cater to different interests and energy levels. Mixing up physical, creative, and discussion-based tasks keeps things interesting and caters to different preferences within the team.
3. **Encourage Collaboration:** Design activities that require collaboration and teamwork. Pairing or grouping team members can foster interaction and ensure that everyone has a role to play. Collaborative tasks promote active engagement and a sense of shared purpose.
4. **Provide Positive Reinforcement:** Acknowledge and celebrate contributions. Positive reinforcement, such as praise or small rewards, can boost morale and encourage continued participation. Recognizing effort and achievement helps build a positive and engaging atmosphere.
5. **Be Adaptable:** Be flexible and ready to adjust the activity if you

notice signs of disengagement. This might mean changing the pace, altering the format, or introducing new elements to re-energize the group. Adaptability ensures that the activity remains relevant and engaging.
6. **Use Interactive Tools:** For virtual teams, leverage interactive tools and platforms to enhance engagement. Use features like polls, breakout rooms, and collaborative boards to keep everyone involved. Interactive tools help replicate the dynamics of in-person interaction in a virtual setting.
7. **Encourage Open Communication:** Foster an environment where team members feel comfortable expressing their thoughts and ideas. Open communication encourages active participation and helps identify any issues or concerns early on. Create opportunities for feedback and discussion throughout the activity.
8. **Monitor and Adjust:** Continuously monitor the group's engagement and be ready to make adjustments. If you notice a drop in participation or enthusiasm, address it promptly. Sometimes a quick break, a change in activity, or a motivational boost can reignite interest and focus.

Successfully performing an activity involves more than just following instructions. It requires active facilitation, keen observation, and a proactive approach to maintaining engagement. By recognizing signs of disengagement and implementing strategies to keep everyone involved, you can ensure that the team building exercise is not only effective but also enjoyable and memorable for all participants. This attention to detail and commitment to engagement will help your team derive maximum benefit from the activity, fostering stronger connections and a more cohesive team dynamic.

Conclusion

By following these initial steps, you set your team up for a successful and impactful team building experience. Analyzing your team's setup, selecting the right activity, reviewing the instructions, and performing the activity with clarity and purpose are all crucial elements in the team building process. With these foundational steps in place, your team is ready to embark on a journey of enhanced cooperation, communication, and creativity.

3

Icebreakers

Icebreakers are a fantastic way to help participants get to know each other and lighten the mood before diving into more intensive team building activities. They create a relaxed and friendly environment, encouraging open communication and breaking down initial barriers. By easing participants into the session, icebreakers help reduce any anxiety or awkwardness, allowing team members to interact more naturally. This relaxed atmosphere is crucial for effective team building, as it fosters an environment where individuals feel comfortable sharing their thoughts and ideas, collaborating openly, and building trust with one another. Icebreakers set the tone for a positive and productive session, paving the way for deeper engagement and more meaningful interactions. Here are five effective icebreakers to kick-start your team building sessions.

Adjective + Name

Objective: Help participants learn each other's names while adding a fun twist that encourages creativity and memory.

Instructions:

1. Gather the team in a circle, either standing or sitting.
2. Ask each participant to think of an adjective that starts with the same letter as their first name. For example, "Happy Hannah" or "Creative Chris."
3. One by one, have each person introduce themselves using their adjective and name.
4. To add a memory challenge, after each new introduction, have the participants repeat the previous names and adjectives in order. For instance, if Chris introduces himself after Hannah, he would say "Happy Hannah, Creative Chris."

Benefits:

- Encourages creativity and fun.
- Helps with name recall through repetition.
- Creates a light-hearted atmosphere.

Two Truths & One Lie

Objective: Encourage participants to share interesting facts about themselves, fostering connections and building trust.

Instructions:

1. Have each participant come up with three statements about themselves: two that are true and one that is a lie.
2. One by one, participants share their three statements with the group.
3. The rest of the group guesses which statement is the lie.
4. After guesses are made, the participant reveals the lie and provides more context or stories about the truths.

Benefits:

- Encourages sharing of personal stories and interests.
- Sparks curiosity and conversation.
- Helps participants learn unique facts about each other.

Introduction Bingo

Objective: Promote interaction and conversation among participants in a fun and engaging way.

Instructions:

1. Create bingo cards with various personal and professional attributes or experiences (e.g., "Has traveled to more than five countries," "Plays a musical instrument," "Has worked here for more than five years").
2. Distribute the bingo cards and pens to participants.
3. Instruct participants to mingle and find colleagues who match the

attributes on their cards, writing down their names.
4. The first person to complete a row or column yells "Bingo!" and shares their findings with the group.

Benefits:

- Encourages mingling and conversation.
- Helps participants discover commonalities and unique traits.
- Adds an element of friendly competition.

The Memory Test

Objective: Enhance memory skills and encourage attentive listening among participants.

Instructions:

1. Form a circle with all participants.
2. Start by having one person say their name and a simple fact about themselves (e.g., "My name is Sarah, and I love hiking").
3. The next person repeats the previous participant's name and fact, then adds their own (e.g., "This is Sarah who loves hiking, and I'm Tom, and I enjoy painting").
4. Continue around the circle, with each new person repeating all previous names and facts before adding their own.
5. The last person will have to recall all the names and facts of the group.

Benefits:

- Develops listening and memory skills.
- Encourages participants to pay close attention to each other.
- Creates a cumulative sense of team identity.

Minefield

Objective: Build trust and enhance communication skills in a fun, physical activity.

Instructions:

1. Set up a "minefield" using objects like cones, chairs, or other small items scattered around an open space.
2. Pair participants and blindfold one person in each pair.
3. The blindfolded person stands at one end of the minefield, and their partner stands at the opposite end.
4. The sighted partner must guide the blindfolded person through the minefield using only verbal instructions.
5. Once across, switch roles and repeat the activity.

Benefits:

- Strengthens trust and reliance on teammates.
- Enhances verbal communication skills.
- Provides a fun and slightly challenging physical activity.

These icebreakers are designed to create an enjoyable and relaxed atmosphere, setting the stage for more intensive team building activities. By helping participants get to know each other and feel more comfortable, these activities pave the way for effective cooperation, communication, and creativity.

4

Team Building Activities to Promote Communication

Effective communication is the cornerstone of any successful team. It ensures that ideas are clearly expressed, misunderstandings are minimized, and collaboration is seamless. When communication flows smoothly, team members can coordinate their efforts efficiently, make informed decisions, and work towards common goals with clarity. This open exchange of information fosters a positive and productive work environment, where everyone feels heard and valued.

The importance of robust communication cannot be overstated. It helps in aligning team goals, sharing critical feedback, and resolving conflicts constructively. Clear communication promotes mutual understanding and trust, which are essential for building strong working relationships. It enables teams to navigate challenges effectively, adapt to changes, and innovate collectively.

Conversely, communication breakdowns pose significant risks to an organization. Poor communication can lead to misunderstandings, which may result in errors, duplicated efforts, and missed opportunities. It can create confusion and frustration among team members, eroding trust and damaging morale. In severe cases, communication issues can lead to conflict, reduced productivity, and ultimately, a negative impact on the organization's overall performance and success.

To mitigate these risks, it is crucial to invest in activities that promote and enhance communication skills. This chapter lists five team building activities designed to promote communication within your team, enhancing their ability to convey and understand information effectively. By practicing these activities, team members will develop stronger communication skills, leading to more effective collaboration and a healthier, more productive work environment.

Can You Hear Me Now?

Objective: Improve verbal communication and active listening skills.

Instructions:

1. Divide participants into small groups. In a virtual setting this can be done in breakout rooms.
2. Give one person in each group a simple image or object that the others cannot see.
3. The person with the image describes it verbally, and the others must draw it based solely on the description.
4. The goal is for teammates to guess the image or object before the drawing is completed.
5. After a set time, reveal the original image.

Benefits:

- Enhances descriptive communication and clarity.

- Develops active listening skills.
- Highlights the importance of clear instructions and feedback.

Blind Drawing

Objective: Strengthen verbal communication and build trust between team members.

Instructions:

1. Divide participants into pairs and provide each pair with paper and pens.
2. One person in each pair is blindfolded or closes their eyes.
3. The sighted person describes an image or object without naming it, and the blindfolded person attempts to draw it based on the description.
4. After the drawing is completed, remove the blindfold and compare the drawing to the described image.

Benefits:

- Encourages precise and effective communication.
- Builds trust between team members.
- Promotes active listening and interpretation skills.

Active Listening

Objective: Enhance listening skills and ensure accurate understanding of messages.

Instructions:

1. Form small groups and present a topic or problem for discussion.
2. Each participant takes turns speaking, while others practice active listening.
3. After each speaker finishes, listeners summarize what was said before adding their thoughts or responses.
4. Continue the discussion, ensuring everyone practices active listening and summarizing.

Benefits:

- Reinforces the importance of listening before responding.
- Ensures accurate understanding and interpretation of messages.
- Fosters a supportive and attentive communication environment.

Spread The Word

Objective: Improve the clarity and efficiency of verbal communication within a team.

Instructions:

1. Create a list of messages or phrases related to your work environ-

ment.
2. Arrange participants in a line or circle.
3. Whisper the message to the first person, who then whispers it to the next, and so on.
4. The last person says the message out loud, and the original message is revealed.
5. Compare the final message to the original and discuss any changes or distortions.

Benefits:

- Highlights the potential for miscommunication.
- Emphasizes the importance of clear and concise messaging.
- Demonstrates how easily information can be altered through poor communication.

Role Play

Objective: Develop empathy, understanding, and effective communication strategies.

Instructions:

1. Create scenarios that are relevant to your team's work environment, such as handling a difficult client, resolving a team conflict, or leading a project meeting.
2. Assign roles to participants and provide them with a brief description of their character and objectives.
3. Allow participants time to prepare, then act out the scenarios.

4. After each role play, conduct a debriefing session to discuss what went well, what could be improved, and what communication strategies were effective.

Benefits:

- Enhances empathy and understanding by seeing situations from different perspectives.
- Provides a safe environment to practice and refine communication strategies.
- Encourages constructive feedback and continuous improvement.

These activities are designed to create a strong foundation for effective communication within your team. By practicing and refining these skills, team members will be better equipped to convey their ideas clearly, listen actively, and collaborate more effectively, ultimately leading to a more cohesive and productive team.

5

Team Building Activities to Promote Cooperation

Cooperation is essential for a team to function effectively and achieve its goals. It involves working together harmoniously, leveraging each other's strengths, and supporting one another to overcome challenges. When team members cooperate, they pool their skills and knowledge, creating a collective capability that far exceeds what individuals could achieve alone. This synergy not only enhances problem-solving and innovation but also drives the team toward achieving shared objectives.

Moreover, cooperation fosters a sense of belonging and commitment within the team. When individuals work together and support each other, they develop a stronger connection to the team and its goals. This sense of belonging is crucial for motivating team members to invest in the success of the organization. It helps them feel valued and integral to the team's achievements, which can lead to increased job satisfaction, higher engagement, and a stronger commitment to the organization's success.

A cooperative team environment encourages open communication, trust, and mutual respect, which are fundamental for building a positive organizational culture. By promoting cooperation, you not only improve the team's ability to meet its goals but also create a supportive and inclusive work environment where everyone feels empowered and motivated to contribute their best efforts.

This chapter introduces five team building activities specifically designed to promote cooperation within your team. These activities are aimed at fostering a collaborative spirit, enhancing collective problem-solving skills, and strengthening the bonds between team members. By engaging in these exercises, your team will develop the skills and mindset necessary to work together effectively, achieve shared goals, and build a more cohesive and invested team.

Visit An Escape Room or Create a Virtual Escape Room

Objective: Encourage teamwork and collaborative problem-solving in a fun and engaging environment.

Instructions:

1. **Visit an Escape Room:**

- Arrange for your team to visit a physical escape room, where they will work together to solve puzzles and complete challenges within a set time limit.
- Ensure that everyone understands the escape room's objective and rules before starting.

1. **Create a Virtual Escape Room:**

- Design a virtual escape room using online platforms or tools that offer interactive puzzles and scenarios.
- Divide the team into smaller groups and have them work together to solve the puzzles and escape the virtual room.

Benefits:

- Promotes teamwork and collective problem-solving.
- Encourages communication and collaboration under pressure.
- Provides a fun and immersive experience that reinforces the value of working together.

Deserted Island

Objective: Foster collaboration and decision-making by prioritizing needs and resources as a team.

Instructions:

1. Present the scenario: your team is stranded on a deserted island with a limited list of items.
2. Each member must choose a few items from the list that they believe are essential for survival.
3. As a group, discuss and negotiate which items to prioritize and create a plan for survival.
4. The team must come to a consensus on the final list of items and justify their choices.

Benefits:

- Encourages collaborative decision-making and negotiation.
- Enhances problem-solving and prioritization skills.
- Fosters a sense of shared responsibility and teamwork.

Question and Answer Board

Objective: Promote cooperation and information sharing through a collaborative Q&A session.

Instructions:

1. Set up a board or digital platform where team members can post questions and answers.
2. Encourage team members to ask questions about work-related topics, challenges, or areas where they seek advice.
3. Each member responds to questions and provides answers based on their expertise and experience.
4. Review the answers as a group and discuss any insights or solutions that arise.

Benefits:

- Facilitates knowledge sharing and collaboration.
- Encourages team members to seek and provide help.
- Strengthens relationships through mutual support and information exchange.

Scavenger Hunt

Objective: Enhance teamwork and problem-solving skills through collaborative and interactive activities.

Instructions:

1. Organize a scavenger hunt with a list of items or clues related to your workplace or team's objectives.
2. Divide the team into smaller groups and provide each group with the scavenger hunt list.
3. Set a time limit for the activity and have the teams work together to find the items or solve the clues.
4. The first team to complete the scavenger hunt wins.

Benefits:

- Encourages teamwork and collaborative problem-solving.
- Enhances team members' ability to work together under time constraints.
- Provides a fun and engaging way to reinforce cooperative skills.

Movie Quote Trivia

Objective: Foster teamwork and collaboration through a fun and competitive trivia game.

Instructions:

TEAM BUILDING ACTIVITIES TO PROMOTE COOPERATION

1. Prepare a list of famous movie quotes from a variety of genres and eras.
2. Divide the team into smaller groups and ask each group to identify the movie from which the quote is taken.
3. Award points for correct answers and keep track of scores throughout the game.
4. Discuss the quotes and their significance to create a light-hearted and collaborative atmosphere.

Benefits:

- Encourages team members to collaborate and share knowledge.
- Provides a fun and relaxed environment for team bonding.
- Reinforces teamwork through friendly competition and shared interests.

These activities are designed to promote cooperation by encouraging team members to work together, make collective decisions, and support each other. By engaging in these collaborative exercises, teams can strengthen their cooperative skills, enhance their ability to work together effectively, and build a more cohesive and productive team environment.

6

Team Building Activities to Inspire Creativity

Creativity is a powerful driver of innovation and problem-solving within a team. Encouraging creative thinking can lead to novel solutions, fresh perspectives, and a more dynamic approach to achieving goals. By fostering an environment where creativity is valued and nurtured, organizations can unlock new opportunities, stay ahead of the competition, and continuously improve their processes and products.

Fostering innovation and creativity is crucial for several reasons. For employees, it enhances job satisfaction and engagement by providing opportunities to express their ideas, contribute to meaningful projects, and be part of a forward-thinking team. Creative environments encourage personal growth and development, allowing employees to explore their talents, take on new challenges, and gain a sense of accomplishment from their contributions.

For organizations, the benefits of fostering creativity are substantial. Creative teams are better equipped to adapt to changes, solve complex problems, and develop innovative products and services. This adaptability helps organizations stay competitive in a rapidly evolving market. Additionally, a culture of creativity attracts top talent who seek dynamic and stimulating work environments, thereby enhancing the organization's overall performance and success.

This chapter introduces five team building activities specifically designed to inspire creativity, foster imaginative thinking, and encourage innovative collaboration among team members. By engaging in these activities, your team will develop creative problem-solving skills, generate fresh ideas, and build a more dynamic and productive work environment. These exercises not only stimulate individual creativity but also strengthen the collective creative potential of the team, leading to a more innovative and successful organization.

Building Block Challenge

Objective: Stimulate creativity and teamwork by constructing a design using limited resources.

Instructions:

1. Provide each team with a set of building blocks or similar materials.
2. Assign a specific challenge or theme (e.g., build a structure that represents your team's goals and values or build the tallest and most stable tower).
3. Set a time limit for the construction and encourage teams to collaborate on their design.
4. After the time is up, have each team present their creation and explain how it relates to the assigned theme.

Benefits:

- Encourages imaginative problem-solving and design thinking.
- Promotes teamwork and collaborative effort.
- Allows for creative expression and showcases diverse ideas.

Paper Plane Contest

Objective: Enhance creativity and experimentation through a competitive yet fun activity.

Instructions:

1. Provide each participant with a sheet of paper and instructions for making paper planes.
2. Allow participants time to design and build their own paper planes.
3. Set up a competition to see whose plane can fly the farthest or achieve specific flight patterns.
4. After the contest, discuss the different designs and approaches used by participants.

Benefits:

- Fosters creative experimentation and innovation.
- Encourages friendly competition and team engagement.
- Provides a tangible and fun way to explore design principles.

Team Goals Collage Board

Objective: Inspire creativity and vision by creating a visual representation of team goals and aspirations.

Instructions:

1. Provide materials such as magazines, scissors, glue, and large poster boards.
2. Have each team create a collage that represents their collective goals, values, and aspirations.
3. Encourage teams to use images, words, and symbols that reflect their vision.
4. After completing the collages, each team presents their board and explains the significance of their chosen elements.

Benefits:

- Enhances visual and conceptual thinking.
- Encourages collaboration and alignment on team goals.
- Creates a shared visual representation of aspirations and values.

What's in the Box

Objective: Stimulate creative thinking and problem-solving by working with unexpected materials.

Instructions:

1. Prepare boxes containing a variety of random items or materials (e.g., paper clips, rubber bands, cardboard).
2. Divide participants into teams and provide each team with a box of materials.
3. Challenge teams to create a functional or artistic object using only the items in their box.
4. Allow time for construction and then have each team present their creation and its purpose.

Benefits:

- Encourages creative problem-solving with limited resources.
- Promotes teamwork and resourcefulness.
- Provides an opportunity for out-of-the-box thinking and innovation.

Back to the Old Drawing Board

Objective: Reignite creativity and innovation by revisiting and reimagining past ideas or solutions.

Instructions:

1. Have each team select a previous project or idea that was not fully realized or faced challenges.
2. Ask teams to review and analyze the old concept, identifying areas for improvement or new approaches.
3. Encourage teams to brainstorm and develop a revised or innovative version of the idea.

4. Present the new ideas and discuss how the reimagined concepts address the original challenges.

Benefits:

- Encourages reflection and improvement of past ideas.
- Fosters a culture of continuous innovation and adaptation.
- Promotes collaborative brainstorming and creative refinement.

These activities are designed to inspire and harness creativity within your team. By engaging in these exercises, team members will be encouraged to think outside the box, collaborate on imaginative projects, and develop innovative solutions, ultimately leading to a more creative and dynamic team environment.

7

Conclusion

As we conclude *Easy Team Building: Activities to Inspire Creativity, Cooperation and Communication*, I hope you now feel equipped and inspired to implement the strategies and activities covered in this guide. The journey towards building a stronger, more cohesive team is both rewarding and crucial for organizational success. By fostering effective communication, enhancing cooperation, and sparking creativity, you are laying the groundwork for a more engaged and high-performing team.

Remember, the principles and activities outlined in this book are designed to be adaptable to your team's unique needs and goals. Whether you're introducing icebreakers to set a positive tone or implementing creative exercises to drive innovation, the ultimate objective is to create an environment where every team member can thrive and contribute to collective success.

I encourage you to take these ideas and tailor them to fit your team's dynamics. Experiment with different activities and be open to feedback and adjustments. The real impact of these exercises comes from their consistent and thoughtful application. By doing so, you will

CONCLUSION

foster a collaborative culture that not only meets your organizational objectives but also enhances the satisfaction and engagement of your team members.

If you've found this book helpful, I would greatly appreciate your support. Please consider leaving a review on Amazon to share your thoughts and experiences. Your feedback will not only help other leaders and managers find this resource but also allow me to continue providing valuable content for team development.

Thank you for allowing me to be a part of your team-building journey. I wish you the best in creating a dynamic and successful team that truly excels together.

8

References

Alexis, M. (2024, April 17). *21 top team meeting icebreakers.* teambuilding.com. https://teambuilding.com/blog/team-meeting-icebreakers

Bit Tech Labs. (2018, May 24). *25 team building activities that your team will love to play.* https://blog.bit.ai/team-building-activities/

Cserti, R., & Cserti, R. (2024, February 22). *61 Ice breaker Games [That your team won't find cheesy] SessionLab.* https://www.sessionlab.com/blog/icebreaker-games/

Elazami, O. (2024, May 29). *Top 20 meeting icebreakers to engage and activate your team.* Beekast. https://www.beekast.com/blog/20-icebreakers-that-guarantee-memorable-meeting-kickoff/

He, G. (2024, February 12). *14 best Collaboration Games & Activities for teams.* teambuilding.com. https://teambuilding.com/blog/collaboration-games

REFERENCES

OpenAI. (2024). *ChatGPT* (version 4). Retrieved from https://www.open ai.com/chatgpt

OptimistMinds. (2023, October 20). *Communication Icebreakers (7 simple activities) | OptimistMinds.* https://optimistminds.com/communication-icebreakers/

Retreat. (n.d.). *Retreat.* https://www.planretreat.com/blog/80-creative-team-building-activities-for-boosting-workplace-collaboration

Robinson, A. (2023, December 9). *21 Fun communication games for teams.* teambuilding.com. https://teambuilding.com/blog/communication-games

Robinson, A. (2024b, April 30). *33 Fun team building exercises for work (Updated).* teambuilding.com. https://teambuilding.com/blog/team-building-exercises

Smart, J., & Smart, J. (2024, February 8). *43 communication games for teams | SessionLab.* SessionLab. https://www.sessionlab.com/blog/communication-games/

Smart, J., & Smart, J. (2024b, May 20). *221 best icebreaker questions for creating genuine connections | SessionLab.* https://www.sessionlab.com/blog/icebreaker-questions/

S, S. K. (2024, May 17). *10 Team building activities to improve collaboration.* Team Building World. https://teambuildingworld.com/collaboration-activities/

Team, D. (2023, June 25). *Top team building activities for collaboration.*

Daisie Blog. https://blog.daisie.com/50-best-team-building-activities-for-fostering-collaboration-and-creativity/

www.ingramcontent.com/pod-product-compliance
Lightning Source LLC
Chambersburg PA
CBHW072003210526
45479CB00003B/1043